SHETLAND PONIES

by Amanda Parise-Peterson

CAPSTONE PRESS
a capstone imprint

Snap Books are published by Capstone Press,
1710 Roe Crest Drive, North Mankato, Minnesota 56003
www.mycapstone.com

Library of Congress Cataloging-in-Publication Data
Names: Parise-Peterson, Amanda, author. Title: Shetland ponies / by
Amanda Parise-Peterson. Description: North Mankato, Minnesota :
Capstone Press, 2018. | Series: Snap books. Horse breeds | Includes
bibliographical references and index. | Audience: Ages 8 to 14.
Identifiers: LCCN 2017038720 (print) | LCCN 2017053758 (ebook) | ISBN
9781543500462 (eBook PDF) | ISBN 9781543500349 (hardcover) |
ISBN 9781543500400 (pbk.) Subjects: LCSH: Shetland pony--Juvenile
literature. Classification: LCC SF315.2.S5 (ebook) | LCC SF315.2.S5 P268
2018 (print) | DDC 636.1/6--dc23 LC record available at https://lccn.loc.
gov/2017038720"

Editorial Credits
Amy Kortuem, editor
Kayla Rossow, designer
Morgan Walters, media researcher
Kathy McColley, production specialist

Image Credits
Alamy: Diane Randell, 14, PearlBucknall, 19, ZUMA Press Inc, 22; Getty
Images: BSIP, 27; iStockphoto: akrp, 5, kipperfletcher23, 29; Newscom:
akg-images, 7, JRAA/ZDS WENN Photos, 21, 25, Mark Bowler/NHPA/
Photoshot/, 11; Shutterstock: Betty Shelton, 4, blue67design, (floral sketch)
design element throughout, Grigorita Ko, 13, 16, 17, Juliata, (floral) design
element throughout, L. Kramer, (fish scale) design throughout, pirita, 15,
redstone, (paper background) design element throughout, Schlegelfotos,
26, suns07butterfly, (watercolor) design element throughout, symbiot,
1, Taras Vyshnya, 2, 3, thomas, 12, Vera Zinkova, Cover, yod67, (horse
vector) design element; SuperStock: Juniors, 8

Printed and bound in the United States.
042718   000438

TABLE OF CONTENTS

Chapter 1
Hard Times

Shetland ponies are small. Many fully grown Shetlands reach only to the waist of an average-sized adult. But Shetlands are one of the strongest horse breeds for their size. Long ago people used the ponies to pull wagons loaded with supplies. Today Shetlands are popular children's ponies.

Shetland ponies receive their name from the Shetland Islands north of Scotland. Ponies have lived on the Shetland Islands for at least 2,000 years. Nobody knows for certain how the ponies got to the islands.

Today about 1,500 Shetland ponies live on the Shetland Islands.

By the 1600s people living on the islands used the ponies for work. The ponies hauled farm supplies and a material called **peat**. The islanders used peat to heat their homes.

A NEW JOB

In 1842 a change in one of Great Britain's laws made work a way of life for many Shetland ponies. This law banned young children from working in coal mines. Mine owners then began using ponies in mines. They liked Shetlands because the ponies fit into the small spaces of mines. The strong ponies also could pull heavy wagons loaded with coal.

People living on the Shetland Islands shipped thousands of ponies to Great Britain for mining. Most of these "pit ponies" were only let out of the dark, dirty mines once each year. By the late 1800s the islands' population of Shetlands had dropped from 10,000 to 5,000.

FACT
In the 1600s people on the Shetland Islands used hair from the manes and tails of Shetland ponies to make fishing line.

peat—dark brown, partly decayed plant matter that is found in bogs and swamps; peat can be used as fuel

Shetland ponies helped keep children safe during World War II (1939-1945) by pulling them away from dangerous areas in carts.

BREEDING SHETLANDS

Mine owners chose strong Shetlands to work in their mines. Weaker ponies were left behind on the islands. Mine owner Lord Londonderry wanted a better supply of suitable mining ponies. In 1870 he set up a breeding farm on the islands. His **stallion** Jack 16 became an important ancestor of today's Shetlands.

Modern American Shetlands have slender necks and legs.

Shetlands in the United States

People first brought Shetlands to the United States in the 1880s. Soon people began to breed the ponies. Some breeders wanted ponies with an elegant look. They bred tall, slender Shetlands. Over time they created ponies that were less muscular than those from the Shetland Islands. These ponies became known as classic American Shetlands.

People in the United States also bred Shetlands with Hackney ponies. The breeding produced lively, high-stepping ponies. Today these ponies are called modern American Shetlands.

Shetland Registries

In 1888 U.S. Shetland owners formed a **registry** called the American Shetland Pony Club (ASPC). The club kept track of each registered Shetland's ancestry. Since it began the ASPC has registered more than 160,000 ponies.

In 1890 British Shetland pony owners formed the Shetland Pony Stud-Book Society (SPSBS). They registered about 500 ponies. Today the SPSBS registers Shetlands that are descendants of these ponies. It registers about 1,500 to 2,000 **foals** each year.

stallion—an adult male horse that can be used for breeding

registry—an organization that keeps track of the ancestry for horses of a certain breed

foal—a horse that is less than 1 year old

CHAPTER 2

Tough and Tender

Over hundreds of years ponies of the Shetland Islands developed features to handle their living conditions. The ponies' small size helped them survive on little food. They grew long coats and manes to stay warm during cold winters.

Most modern Shetlands no longer face hard living conditions. But they still share many features of their **ancestors**.

SIZE

Shetland ponies are measured from the ground to the highest point of their shoulders, or withers. They are measured in inches.

ancestor—a member of a breed that lived a long time ago

Many of today's Shetlands
live in large, grassy pastures.

Most Shetlands are between 27 and 42 inches (69 and 107 centimeters) tall. The SPSBS registers only ponies that are 42 inches tall or less at age 4 or older. The ASPC allows Shetlands to be as tall as 46 inches (117 cm).

The smallest Shetlands are called miniature Shetlands. These ponies are 34 inches (86 cm) tall or less at age 4 or older.

BUILD AND COLOR

Small size is just one feature that Shetlands share. Shetlands have rounded bodies and muscular hindquarters. They have short legs and tough, round hooves. Their sloped shoulders lead to a muscular neck. Shetlands have small heads with wide foreheads. They have small ears and large nostrils.

Shetlands can be almost any color. Colors include black, chestnut, gray, bay, and piebald. Chestnut is a copper color. Bay ponies are a shade of brown. They have black manes and tails. Bay ponies also have black coloring on their lower legs. Piebald ponies have black and white patches.

Cremello Shetland ponies are cream, but they can sometimes look white.

WARM COATS

Unlike other horses, Shetland ponies grow double coats in winter. The inside coat is soft. The outer coat is thick. Long hairs called guard hairs keep water from reaching the inside layer. The coat is so protective that snow often lies unmelted on a Shetland's back.

Double coats keep snow from melting on the backs of Shetland ponies.

PERSONALITY

Shetland ponies are gentle. They bond strongly with their owners and handlers. These features make them good ponies for children. Managers of riding programs for children with disabilities often use Shetlands.

The intelligence of Shetland ponies helps them learn quickly. Some Shetlands learn tricks that they perform in circuses. They may learn to rear, walk on their hind legs, or perform with other animals.

FACT

Like the Shetland pony, other animals from the Shetland Islands are small with thick coats. These animals include Shetland sheepdogs and Shetland sheep.

muscular hindquarters

short legs

thick mane

small ears

wide forehead

large nostrils

sloped shoulders

Chapter 3

A Show Pony for Everyone

By the 1950s machines had replaced Shetland ponies in coal mines. People then kept Shetlands as pets and as children's ponies. Some owners competed with their ponies at shows. Shetlands were strong competitors against larger horse breeds. Today the ponies compete at all-Shetland events and at shows with other breeds.

Shetlands are popular show ponies for children.

PERFORMANCE AWARD SCHEME

The United Kingdom is home to many all-Shetland competitions. The most popular events are part of the Performance Award Scheme. Members of the SPSBS started the scheme in 1980. Riders 8 to 13 years old compete in the scheme.

Scheme events include lead rein, **dressage**, and **gymkhana**. In lead rein, a handler leads a pony while a young child rides it. Riders competing in dressage guide their ponies through a series of advanced moves. Ponies may step sideways or turn while keeping their front legs in place. Gymkhana is a combination of games that test the skills of ponies and riders. Gymkhana ponies must be fast and easy to control.

Riders earn points at each Performance Award Scheme event. At the end of the season, the rider with the most points receives the Nan French trophy.

dressage—a riding style in which horses complete a pattern while doing advanced moves

gymkhana—a combination of competitive games on horseback

Shetland Pony Grand National

Some riders in the Performance Award Scheme also compete in the Shetland Pony Grand National. This event is held each December during the Olympia International Horse Show in London, England. It is based on the famous Grand National race for adult riders.

At the Shetland Grand National, riders jump over brush fences that are about 2 feet (.6 meter) high. The rider who completes the jumps the fastest wins.

The Shetland Grand National raises money for charities. The event has raised hundreds of thousands of dollars since it started in 1982.

The American Shetland Pony Club sets up rules for most Shetland shows in the United States. Ponies that participate in these ASPC-sanctioned shows must be registered by the ASPC.

Owners begin working with American Shetlands when the ponies are young.

Most shows include **halter**, riding, and **harness** classes. In halter classes handlers lead their ponies around the ring. Judges score the ponies on their physical features. Ponies pull carts in harness classes.

Each year the ASPC holds the Shetland Congress. Ponies that win at the show receive national champion titles. In 2017 about 700 ponies competed at the Shetland Congress.

FACT

More Shetland ponies live on the Scottish island of Foula than people do. Foula Island is said to be where the Shetland breed began thousands of years ago. There are 50 ponies to every one human living on Foula.

TRAINING SHETLANDS

People train Shetland ponies much like they train larger horses. Many Shetland breeders begin handling a foal right after it is born. After a few months, trainers fit a halter around a pony's head. They teach the pony to lead. By age 4 Shetlands usually are strong enough to be ridden.

halter—a rope or strap used to lead a horse; the halter fits over the horse's nose and behind its ears

harness—a set of leather straps and metal pieces that connect a horse to a cart

Chapter 4

Shetlands in Action

Shetlands are competitive at events other than shows. In the midwestern United States, people compete with their Shetlands in pulling contests. Ponies that pull the heaviest loads win the events.

Strong legs give Shetland ponies good jumping abilities. Some Shetlands jump at the U.S. Equestrian National Pony Hunter Championships that are held each year.

FACT

Madame Nou, the world's oldest Shetland pony, died in 2013 at the age of 50. That's 30 years longer than the average Shetland life span. About 1,500 children learned to ride on Madame Nou.

Shetland ponies have natural jumping abilities.

CARE

Caring for Shetlands is slightly different from taking care of other horses. Shetland ponies are hardy. They can handle cold weather better than other horses can.

Shetlands rarely need as much food as other ponies. Many people feed ponies both hay and grain. Shetlands usually need only pasture grass or hay. Shetlands that eat too much can develop a foot disease called **laminitis**.

Most Shetlands need only pasture grass to eat.

laminitis–a painful hoof disease of horses

Shetlands have tough feet. But they still need their hooves trimmed regularly. Some ponies wear shoes to protect their feet.

Shetland owners throughout the world treasure their strong, talented ponies. Shetlands are sure to remain one of the world's most popular pony breeds for years to come.

Personal Ponies

In 1986 a horse breeder named Marianne Alexander formed an organization called Personal Ponies. Her dream was to bring ponies and children with disabilities together. She brought Shetlands from the United Kingdom to the United States and started a breeding program. She chose Shetlands because they are gentle and patient around children. Today Personal Ponies is a national organization that places ponies in therapy centers and community programs. It has Shetlands serving people of all ages in almost every state.

Fast Facts:
The Shetland Pony

Name: Shetland ponies are named for the Shetland Islands.

History: Shetland ponies have lived on the Shetland Islands for thousands of years. In the 1800s people shipped many Shetlands to Great Britain and the United States.

Height: Shetland ponies usually stand between 27 and 42 inches (69 and 107 centimeters) tall at the withers. Some American Shetlands are as tall as 46 inches (117 centimeters).

Weight: Shetland ponies usually weigh between 300 and 450 pounds (140 and 200 kilograms).

Colors: Shetlands can be almost any color. Common colors are black, chestnut, gray, bay, and brown.

Features: small head; small ears; wide forehead; thick mane; large nostrils; rounded body; strong hindquarters; thick double winter coats; tough hooves

Personality: gentle, intelligent, independent

Abilities: Shetlands compete at shows in harness, riding, and halter classes. They also have good jumping abilities.

Life span: about 20 to 25 years

Glossary

ancestor (AN-sess-tur)–a member of a breed that lived a long time ago

dressage (druh-SAHJ)–a riding style in which horses complete a pattern while doing advanced moves

foal (FOHL)–a horse that is less than 1 year old

gymkhana (jim-KAH-nuh)–a combination of competitive games on horseback

halter (HAWL-tur)–a rope or strap used to lead a horse; the halter fits over the horse's nose and behind its ears

harness (HAR-niss)–a set of leather straps and metal pieces that connect a horse to a cart

laminitis (lah-muh-NYE-tuhss)–a painful hoof disease of horses

peat (PEET)–dark brown, partly decayed plant matter that is found in bogs and swamps; peat can be used as fuel

registry (REH-juh-stree)–an organization that keeps track of the ancestry for horses of a certain breed

stallion (STAL-yuhn)–an adult male horse that can be used for breeding

Read More

Dell, Pamela. *Shetland Ponies.* Majestic Horses. North Mankato, Minn.: Child's World, Inc., 2014.

Kolpin, Molly. *Favorite Horses: Breeds Girls Love.* Crazy About Horses. North Mankato, Minn.: Capstone Press, 2015.

Osborne, Mary Pope, and Natalie Pope Boyce. *Horse Heroes.* Magic Tree House Fact Tracker. Bel Air, Calif.: Random House for Young Readers, 2013.

Internet Sites

Use FactHound to find Internet sites related to this book.

Visit *www.facthound.com*

Just type in 9781543500349 and go.

Super-cool stuff! Check out projects, games and lots more at www.capstonekids.com

Index